KU-863-327

OTEGHA UWAGBA

LITTLE BLACK BOOK

A TOOLKIT FOR WORKING WOMEN

4th Estate • London

4th Estate
An imprint of HarperCollins*Publishers*
1 London Bridge Street, London SE1 9GF

www.4thEstate.co.uk

First published in Great Britain in 2016
This edition published by 4th Estate in 2017

1

A catalogue record for this book is available from the British Library

ISBN 978-0-00-824511-5

Set in Adobe Garamond

Printed and bound in Great Britain by Clays Ltd, St Ives plc

FSC™ is a non-profit international organisation established to promote the responsible
management of the world's forests. Products carrying the FSC label are independently certified
to assure consumers that they come from forests that are managed to meet the social, economic
and ecological needs of present and future generations, and other controlled sources.

Find out more about HarperCollins and the environment at
www.harpercollins.co.uk

Dedicated to my parents,
who taught me the meaning of hard work,
and continue to lead by example.

CONTENTS

FOREWORD

If you're a working woman and you've picked up this book, it's probably because you've got some questions. Maybe you're just starting out, or maybe you're already pretty experienced. Still, you've got questions. You're in the right place – read on.

The book you're holding right now is a curation of career advice and insights inspired by my own experiences as a young woman trying to make my way in the world. Despite having been lucky enough to start my career at some of the world's top ad agencies, and later working for cult youth brand Vice, after a few years I found myself at something of a career crossroads: completely unsure of what to do next, but knowing deep down that I needed to make a change – sound familiar?

Feeling certain my own experiences couldn't be unique, and desperate to connect with other like-minded women, I decided to combine the things I'm most inspired by – creativity, women and work – into a platform that could support and inspire working women everywhere. Enter Women Who: a modern community connecting women who, separately, are all having the same thoughts when they wake up in the morning. Women who are striving for more. Women who, like me, want – or need – to make a change.

Because things *are* changing, aren't they? The offices, studios and coffee shops where we spend the majority of our waking hours are constantly evolving, and with them the rulebook on how to build a successful and fulfilling creative career. For the generation of fiercely ambitious and entrepreneurial women that I'm a part of, navigating that ever-changing landscape throws up a bunch of complex questions – from little things like how to write a sensitive email, or use Instagram to your advantage; to the big, existential, career-defining quandaries, like how to build the kind of personal brand that opens doors, whether to try free-lancing or not, and of course, the lifelong dilemma every creative faces – how to find that delicate balance between starving artist and corporate shill.

All of which brings us right back to this book, which I wrote to help answer all of those questions (and a few more besides), and to show you how you can achieve success on your own terms – whatever those may be.

Because if there's one thing I've learned along the way, it's that we all *have* ideas – sometimes we just need a little help figuring out how to make them happen.

So – let's get to work, shall we?

Otegha x

To find out more about Women Who visit www.womenwho.co or follow @womenwho on Instagram, Twitter and Facebook.

Chapter 1

GETTING IT DONE

WAYS TO MAXIMIZE YOUR PRODUCTIVITY

'Nothing will work unless you do.'
– Maya Angelou, poet and activist

Producing creative work often means juggling a seemingly endless number of deadlines and projects. This can be both a blessing and a curse: while a bit of variety keeps things fresh, good time management is infinitely trickier when you have lots of competing demands on your time. Read on for some effective ways to make the most of your working hours.

THE EARLY BIRD

Try starting your working day an hour earlier. If you're not used to early starts this will probably be a little painful at first, but you'll soon notice the benefits of getting a head start on your work without anyone to disrupt you, especially if you have clients to report to. Consistency is key to making this habit stick, which means getting up at the same time every day. Studies have also shown that people who get up early actually tend to have *higher* energy levels, and feel more in control of their day – even more reason to become a morning person. And on that note . . .

POWER HOUR

Resist the temptation to check your emails or social media accounts first thing in the morning, as you run the risk of falling down an Internet rabbit hole. Instead, dedicate the first hour of your working day – when your mind is at its freshest – to establishing what your priorities are for the day ahead and making a start on them. That first hour is precious, so make the most of it.

GETTING DRESSED

Many world leaders and CEOs swear by having a 'work uniform', i.e. returning to the same outfit (or variations thereof) day in, day out. Eliminating smaller choices such as what to wear each morning means one fewer decision to make over the course of your day, so you can save your brainpower for the important stuff. Plus, you'll save precious minutes in the morning, which can only be a good thing.

Having a consistent look is also a great way of establishing your personal brand – find out more about that in Chapter 3.

MAKE A LIST

Despite the many wonders of modern technology, the humble list remains one of the most effective productivity power tools at your disposal. At the start of each week, make a to-do list of your key goals for the week ahead, prioritizing them in order of importance. By spending a few minutes planning your workflow upfront, you free your brain up to do the *real* work of creative thinking the rest of the time. You might also find it helps to go analogue with this – the process of committing your thoughts to paper can be incredibly clarifying, and having a written list to hand means your goals won't get lost in the jumble of draft tweets and browser tabs that tend to dominate our lives.

QUALITY OVER QUANTITY

Working non-stop doesn't necessarily equate to getting more done, as your brain simply can't operate at peak performance for long stretches of time. Instead of trying to work marathon sessions, aim for shorter periods of focused activity interspersed with regular breaks allowing your brain to recharge. Try scheduling your day into a few two-hour 'work blocks', comprised of ninety minutes of work followed by a thirty-minute break. Resist the temptation to carry on working beyond the allotted time for each block just because you're 'in the zone' – you'll be more motivated to return to work if there's something you're dying to finish, as opposed to working yourself to the point of exhaustion.

ONE THING AT A TIME

Multitasking is overrated! If you've got several projects on the go, it's easy to get distracted by flitting from one project to another but that's an exhausting way of working, and one that reduces your efficiency. Don't fracture your time by jumping from task to task – pick one task you want to complete in a given time slot (e.g. one or more work blocks) and focus on just that.

PEAK TIME

Identify your most productive times of day – are you an early bird or a night owl? It's natural for your energy levels to fluctuate throughout the day, so figure out the time of day when your focus tends to be at its peak and schedule important tasks for then. Try starting with the most difficult task on your to-do list first. The sense of accomplishment (and relief) from having ticked it off your list will give you a burst of energy that propels you through the rest of your day.

LUNCHTIME

Avoid a hastily gobbled lunch 'al desko', and always aim to take a full hour for your lunch break if possible. At the very least, make sure you're well away from your phone or computer when eating your lunch – this is your time to recharge your brain so don't try and multitask. If you can manage it, take a quick walk outside, too. A few minutes of fresh air will do wonders for your energy levels and sense of calm.

COMPARTMENTALIZE

Relegate emails, admin and social media activity to specific times of the day, factoring in your 'peak energy' hours and working around them. If you need to, consider switching the notifications settings on your phone from push to pull, to avoid the distraction – and temptation – of notifications popping up. Frequently interrupting your work to check or respond to messages stops you from getting properly immersed in it, as it takes the average person around twenty-five minutes to get back into the swing of things after a distraction. The same principle applies to 'life admin' such as going to the supermarket or doing housework – set aside a regular slot once or twice a week to deal with everything in one go. Knowing you have a pre-allocated time to tackle these tasks will also help you put them to the back of your mind and concentrate better the rest of the time.

THINK IT OVER

It's easy to feel as though constant busyness is the ultimate indicator of productivity, but making time for 'deep thinking' is just as essential to your output as ticking items off your daily to-do list. Try to block out at least one hour-long slot in your diary every week just to think, strategize and evaluate how you're working. That might feel like something of a luxury in the face of the endless demands on your plate, but taking the time to clarify your priorities, think about how you're expending your energy and generate new ideas is a vital investment in making long-term headway on your goals.

SET DEADLINES

Having an actual deadline can improve your performance and reduce your tendency to procrastinate no end, so as you begin each task allocate yourself a set amount of time within which to finish it. Make sure the deadline is achievable and allows enough time to get the job done well – don't subject yourself to unnecessary pressure by setting unrealistic goals. Not allowing tasks to expand to fit the time available to you is a crucial habit to cultivate, and it's even more salient if you're a freelancer and your time is, quite literally, money.

DONE IS BETTER THAN PERFECT

Perfectionism is very often the enemy of progress. Resist the urge to endlessly tweak projects or creative work at the expense of ever actually finishing them. Following through – even if you're not 100 per cent happy with the final product – is more valuable than endlessly chasing an unattainable ideal of 'perfection'. Recognize where to draw the line and put your work out into the world. After all, if no one ever sees your work, then it doesn't really exist, does it?

Chapter 2

OVERCOMING CREATIVE BLOCKS

GETTING YOUR MOJO BACK

'Show up, show up, show up, and after
a while, the muse shows up, too.'
– Isabel Allende, writer

Everyone struggles with creative block from time to time, and finding that your ideas come less easily at some points than at others is pretty much part and parcel of doing creative work. Still, when your livelihood depends on your ability to generate ideas, going through a creative dry spell is far from ideal. Whether you're dealing with a seemingly impenetrable brief, or having trouble going from idea to execution, here are a few simple strategies to help you get your work back on track.

LOOK OUTSIDE YOUR GENRE

Your best ideas won't always come to you when you're sitting at your desk, so get out there and find fresh sources of inspiration. Whether it's going to a talk, reading a book, or travelling somewhere new, putting yourself in a position to absorb information from outside your usual frames of reference is great for sparking new ideas, and developing work that reflects your own unique range of inspirations.

DON'T SURROUND YOURSELF WITH YOURSELF

Don't be afraid to open your work process up to others – if you've hit a wall, talking things through with someone else can really help. It's a simple but often overlooked truth that a fresh pair of eyes usually helps you look at problems from a different perspective. No woman is an island, so open up to someone whose opinion or judgement you respect.

PRIORITIZE

On a day-to-day level, simplify your to-do list to make it more manageable. Chances are you'll find you don't have to do everything *right now*, and it's always better to do a few things well than many things badly. Be ruthless in figuring out what you can delay, delegate (if you work in a team), or skip altogether.

ACE YOUR SPACE

Creating the right conditions for inspiration to strike is crucial to doing your best work. Your working environment has a huge impact on your mindset and creativity levels, particularly if you regularly work from home – it needs to be somewhere you're happy to be in for hours on end, day in, day out. It's also far easier to get in the zone (and out of it when your workday's over) if you have a dedicated workspace, no matter how small. Whether you're working from home or based in an office, make sure you've got these basics sorted.

Get organized
Some people swear by organizing their desk every morning before getting down to work, in the belief that a tidy desk equals a tidy mind – or at least helps. Kondo (for the uninitiated, this means declutter) your workspace using desk drawer organizers, folders and filing cabinets, and treat yourself to some cute desk accessories to elevate your workspace beyond the mundane. Muji is a great option if you like your stationery minimal, and cheap.

Go green

Recreate the mood-boosting properties of the great outdoors by sprucing up your workspace with some greenery. If a continual supply of fresh flowers is too much hassle for you, go for an easy-to-care-for succulent such as aloe vera, which has the added bonus of purifying the air around you.

Lighting

Ensure you're working in a well-lit environment – if you can work somewhere with plenty of natural light, all the better.

Make your space unique

Adding some personal touches to your workspace by pinning up a few pictures, postcards, or inspirational quotes can do wonders for keeping you motivated when you've hit a wall.

Get comfortable

Your workspace should be as conducive to comfort as possible – if you're uncomfortable, you won't be able to concentrate properly, particularly on those days when you need to put in long hours. Make sure your computer screen is at the right height, and that you've got a chair with good back support. If you use a laptop, get an external mouse instead of relying on its touchpad; over time that can strain your hands and wrists.

Tune in
Music can go a long way towards creating the right ambience for your workspace, so experiment a little to see what works for you. Or you could take a leaf out of writer Zadie Smith's book: she listens to 'brown noise' (like white noise, but more soothing) as she works. Unconventional, sure – but it's great for drowning out distracting thoughts and sounds, and you might find that avoiding music with words or a distinct melody while working is less distracting. If you work in a busy office, make sure you've got a decent pair of noise-cancelling headphones on hand for those times when you really need to power through.

CHANGE YOUR SCENERY
Don't forget to mix it up once in a while. If you usually work from home, try to spend one or two days a week working in a different environment, whether it's your local library, a dedicated co-working space or a chilled-out café (check out the Appendix for some freelancer-friendly workspaces around the world). If you work in an office, try working in a different part

of the office or from a communal area. Staring at the same four walls day in, day out has a tendency to make your mind stagnate, so switch it up!

BREAK IT UP

If you're feeling truly stuck, step away from what you're doing; forcing yourself to power through will only lead to mediocre work. Either focus on another task for a while, or stop working altogether and come back to the original block a little while later. Completely immersing yourself in work 24/7 doesn't necessarily mean you'll produce your best work, or even more of it.

DIGITAL DETOX

Try going 'screen-free' by switching off your phone and laptop for a few hours of each workday. You'll be surprised at how much more you can get done without the constant distraction of digital technology at your fingertips. Often your best thinking happens with a pen in hand, so put the screens away and go old-school.

CUT THE CRAP

Every now and then, take the time to consciously evaluate the work you're currently doing, and weigh it up against the kind of work you ultimately want to do. Which projects or aspects of your job description do you find most stimulating? Once you've worked this out, make a conscious effort to slowly recalibrate your working life to incorporate more of this type of work. This could involve discussing your role and career development with your boss, or doing more work for certain types of clients. Making a long-term commitment to streamlining your work output so you're doing more of what you find interesting will likely get you feeling more inspired in the long run.

Chapter 3

BUILDING YOUR BRAND

NOT JUST A CORPORATE BUZZWORD – THE IMPORTANCE OF PERSONAL BRANDING

'Always be a first-rate version of yourself and not a second-rate version of someone else.'
– Judy Garland, actress

The integration of social media into pretty much every aspect of our personal and professional lives has made it easier than ever to hone your 'brand'. But what exactly *is* a personal brand? And do you actually need one?

STANDING OUT

Your personal brand is a way of letting people – particularly potential employers or clients – know what your distinct talents are, and what you represent. In industries where competition is fierce and your skills may be easily interchangeable with the next [insert profession here], having a strong personal brand is a way of marketing yourself to others. It's what makes people choose you over the next person, and keeps them coming back for more – besides the quality of your work, which, it goes without saying, needs to be top-notch. Having a solid personal brand can make your job searches a little more fruitful, or help turn your side hustle into more than just a hobby.

And here's the truth: you already *have* a brand. There's already a wealth of information readily available to anyone who chooses to Google you, and it tells a story about you. Being more strategic about that information is a way of controlling the conversation and creating your own narrative, instead of letting others do it for you.

FIND YOUR NICHE

Find and understand your USP (unique selling point). What particular combination of skills do you have that few others can offer? Are you an illustrator who's got a lot of experience working on fashion-related briefs? Or a features writer who also happens to be a dab hand at photography? Communicating the unique qualities you have that set you apart from the competition will pay dividends, whether that means being commissioned on an exciting project, or putting you on the fast track to promotion.

DRESS THE PART

We're judged in a matter of seconds on our appearance, whether at a party or a job interview. It might sound superficial, but your appearance is a crucial part of your brand, as the way you dress has an enormous impact on people's perception of you. Human beings are highly visual creatures, and a strong, consistent aesthetic tends to stick in the memory. This doesn't mean you have to dress in head-to-toe Prada (although if that's your thing, do you). Start by striking a balance between expressing your personality and looking professional, which, depending on where you work, can be anywhere on a sliding scale from tracksuits to power suits. Whatever you wear, make sure it's something that makes you *feel* good – your wardrobe choices influence your mindset, and feeling comfortable and confident about your appearance will translate to your attitude, helping you work better.

STICK TO YOUR GUNS

Values are key, so identify what matters to you and what your ethics are. Do you enjoy social good projects? Working in a collaborative environment? Mentoring others? Figuring out what motivates and excites you (or what annoys and bores you) and being able to convey that to others makes you more than just another face in the crowd. Don't be afraid to be vocal about your passions.

GET SOCIAL

If you work in the creative industries and you're not up on your social media, you're seriously missing a trick. Social media is a fast, easy way to self-promote (something women unfortunately tend to shy away from) and a great way of keeping up with new developments and job opportunities in your industry. It's not necessarily just about having a huge number of followers either – ignore the popularity contest and focus on how social media platforms allow you to give people a taste of your personality and communicate that directly, #nofilter. Be consistent – even little things like using the same profile picture across different platforms make a difference.

SELF-PROMOTE

For freelancers in particular, letting people know about the work you've done for other clients is part of the game – people always want to work with creatives who seem like they're in demand, so don't shy away from plugging your work at events and on social media, or sending it into industry publications for consideration. If you work in an office, make sure your manager *and* your peers are aware of your wins – get comfortable with tooting your own horn!

BE EASY TO FIND

If you have a portfolio-based job, make sure you have a personal website filled with examples of your best work, and the type of work you'd like to do more of. Squarespace's well-designed, easy-to-use templates are a great option if you're not a coding whizz. Be selective about the work you showcase too – quality wins over quantity every time.

STAY CURRENT

Make sure your CV and any online profiles you have are always bang up to date, and don't just wait until you're in the market for a new job. You should update them regularly while your accomplishments are still fresh in your mind, and so any potential employers checking you out online have a clear picture of what you're currently up to. It doesn't hurt to always have a ready-to-go CV either.

GO THE EXTRA MILE

Whether that's writing articles for relevant industry publications, starting a blog, or joining a community of like-minded creatives such as Women Who – it pays to be engaged and to have opinions. If you've got an impressive side hustle, include it on your personal website or CV. Doing something that goes above and beyond your day-to-day work is a great way of boosting your profile, and makes you much more appealing to work with.

KEEP IT REAL

Above all, be authentic. Your personality is the most important part of your brand, so stay true to yourself. Your online persona should be genuinely representative of what you're actually like in person. If your sassy Twitter alter ego turns out to be a timid wallflower IRL, the disparity between the 'real' you and the 'curated' you is only going to be a let-down, which won't work in your favour. Don't let a preoccupation with your 'brand' get in the way of the really important stuff either, or spend more time self-promoting than doing the hard work of actually honing your craft. The best personal brand is being really good at what you do.

Chapter 4

PUBLIC SPEAKING 101

HOW TO GIVE A KICK-ASS PRESENTATION

'I like a good speaker, and I appreciate
an intelligent audience.'
– Dorothy Parker, poet, writer and critic

To thrive in the creative industries, you've gotta give good pitch. Being an effective saleswoman – of your work, of your ideas and of yourself – is one of the most useful skills you can cultivate, which means mastering the art of giving convincing presentations. Read on for some tips and tricks that can be applied in most situations, whether you're giving a talk at an event, or pitching to a prospective client, investor or employer.

WORD COUNT

If you'll be delivering your talk using a slide show, keep the number of words on each slide to an absolute minimum. There's nothing more boring than sitting through a talk where the entire contents are written out on each slide – people *will* tune out of what you're saying and read your presentation off the screen behind you instead. Visuals are a good way of keeping your audience's attention, so (if the subject of your talk allows it) incorporate some eye-catching imagery to support your narrative. Copy-wise, try limiting yourself to brief headings on each slide, and structure your presentation so that the headings of each slide spell out the key points of your presentation. Try it – it's a game-changer.

USING NOTES

Presenting without notes definitely looks slicker and more polished, but they're a good confidence-boosting safety net if you're feeling nervous or haven't had much time to prepare. An occasional glance at your notes is much better than losing your train of thought halfway through your presentation. Just make sure you're holding a few discreet cue cards, not stacks of rustling paper. Jot down key prompts, keywords, or even the beginnings of sentences to jog your memory.

STRUCTURE AND PACE

Introduction, argument, conclusion: treat giving a presentation like writing an essay, and keep all of the sections roughly the same length, with a quick recap at the end to remind your audience of the key points. If you're presenting multiple options for consideration, go into a little more detail on your preferred option – it's a simple but effective psychological trick that can help sway your audience towards your choice, without making them feel as though the decision is being made for them.

LOOKS COUNT

Whatever program you use to create your presentation (Keynote and Google Slides are both good options), ensure your formatting is tight. That means consistent use of font – no more than one or two fonts or font sizes – and sleek, crisp-looking slides. If you're pitching to a major client or potential investor, consider investing in a few hours of a designer's time to make your deck as visually appealing as possible.

KEEP IT SIMPLE

No special effects, please. Nobody wants to watch your slide title crawl, whoosh, or fade onto a page.

PRACTICE MAKES PERFECT

Whether you're new to public speaking or a seasoned pro, rehearse your talk as much as you can, both on your own and in front of willing friends. Learn your presentation inside out, then practise delivering it so you seem relaxed and natural. If you end up feeling comfortable enough to throw in a few ad-libs, that's great too.

ALL KILLER, NO FILLER

Filler words such as 'um', 'er' and 'like' are pretty damn jarring from an audience perspective and make you sound a lot less polished. Try recording yourself giving your presentation on your mobile phone and watching it back – you'll probably be surprised at how often you end up using them. The better you know your presentation, the less likely you'll be left fumbling for the right words and reach for one of these instead – yet another reason to get practising!

BODY TALK

Public speaking can be hugely nerve-racking, especially if it's something you don't do very often, or, worse, have never done before. Feeling nervous often triggers a fight-or-flight response in our bodies, leading to a huge surge of adrenaline that can manifest itself in the form of shaky hands, sweaty armpits, or a dry mouth – not exactly ideal when you're standing in front of an audience! Try the following techniques to help counteract your body's (totally natural) reaction to nerves:

Breathe

A few minutes before you're due to speak, do a bit of meditation-style breathing. Taking slow, deep breaths will give your body a much-needed influx of oxygen, calming you down and helping to alleviate any physical signs of nervousness you might be showing.

Drink water

Make sure you're well hydrated and have a glass of water handy while you're speaking, in case your mouth starts feeling dry. Tempting though it might be to rely on a bit of Dutch courage, you should avoid hitting the booze beforehand. Alcohol dehydrates your body (which won't help with a dry mouth) and impairs your cognitive functioning – which makes you more likely to lose your train of thought, and could slow your responses if there's a Q&A element to your talk. Save the glass of wine for celebrating afterwards!

Eat something
Having an empty stomach can exacerbate your anxiety, so make time for a light snack a good hour or so before your presentation.

EYE CONTACT
Make eye contact with your audience, dividing your attention equally between all corners of the room. Early on in your presentation, try to find friendly-looking faces in the audience and direct your words towards them. They'll make you feel calmer and more confident and help you gauge how your words are going down.

TELL A STORY
The best presentations have a bit of levity, so include a relevant anecdote (personal or otherwise) to humanize yourself and help build a connection with your audience. Stories are a great way to start off a presentation, as they instantly capture people's attention.

WHAT TO WEAR

Dressing with personality is great in general, but this is one situation where you don't want your outfit to distract from what you're saying. So keep it simple.

Any questions?

Chapter 5

MONEY TALKS PART I: KNOWING YOUR WORTH

GETTING PAID WHAT YOU DESERVE

'Civil liberties are theoretical if they are
not accompanied by economic freedom.'
– Simone de Beauvoir, writer and activist

When you do creative work for a living, it can be
all too easy to shy away from the commercial and
financial aspects of working life. The (not entirely
undeserved) notion that the admin involved in dealing with finances is boring, combined with the fairly
'uncreative' nature of money management, tends to
put many people off dealing with it head first. Given
its subjective nature, creative work can also be difficult to quantify, and therefore hard to put a price on
– what *isn't* difficult is finding excuses to talk yourself

out of asking for more money. Not to mention that our general reluctance to talk openly about money in professional settings is further exacerbated within the creative fields, where there's at times a slight snobbishness about money and the notion of 'selling out'. All of this means that it can be hard to know where to begin.

Yet money management, and ensuring you're properly compensated for the work you do, is as much a part of your job as the fun, creative side – particularly if you're self-employed, or want to turn your ideas into a business. Being financially literate is an infinitely powerful thing, especially for women – and it's never too late (or too early) to get your finances in order. You'll probably find that the sense of freedom having a handle on your money brings will actually enable you to do your best work.

So no more excuses. The next two chapters are about how to 'do' money, so you can get – and keep – that paper.

SALARY BENCHMARKS
Finding out where you are on the pay scale can be tricky given the taboo surrounding discussing sal-

aries with friends or co-workers. As a starting point, try tactfully asking around among industry friends, mentors and recruiters to make sure you understand what the going rate is for a given job, company, or freelance gig. Try to check in with people who work in different parts of your industry too, to get a variety of perspectives. Be reasonably upfront about your reasons for asking, and always make it easy for the other person to politely avoid the conversation if they're uncomfortable discussing it. A good way of framing your question is to ask if they'd accept £X salary for a certain position, or to find out what they'd consider a fair figure. It's a bit more diplomatic than asking for someone's salary outright, and you're more likely to get a helpful answer. Online salary surveys can also be useful, but be sure to corroborate your findings with some IRL research to factor in the vagaries of your specific environment.

NEGOTIATING A PAY RISE

Be prepared
Have a benchmark figure in mind, based on similar roles within your company and the wider industry. Try applying Broadly editor Zing Tsjeng's '20 per cent rule' discussed in Chapter 10. What would your

company have to pay a new recruit to entice them into taking your role? Start there.

Timing is key
Set up a proper meeting with your boss, indicating that you'd like to talk about your contribution to the company and future prospects. Make sure you clearly signpost the purpose of the meeting, so your boss has time to prepare as well – nobody likes being blindsided.

Do your homework
Do your due diligence on the whole company's fortunes, not just the issues in your immediate vicinity. Layoffs? New management? Expansion? All of these could be important factors in the timing and success of your request.

Rehearse beforehand
We only negotiate our salaries very rarely, so naturally it tends to be something we're not very well practised at. Rehearse the conversation as much as you can with a willing friend, going over possible pushbacks and counterarguments.

Make your case

Outline what you've contributed to the organization, presenting tangible achievements and quantifiable wins. Avoid emotional language such as 'I want' or 'I need' at all costs, and instead use phrases like 'I've achieved' or 'I deserve'. Frame your request as a business argument, not one stemming from personal desire or need (even if that's the case!). Speak your boss's language at all times.

The power of silence

Once you've made your argument, simply state the figure or range you have in mind and wait for a response. Asking for money tends to make most people feel pretty awkward, but resist the urge to ramble on in order to fill the silence, or provide caveats and further justifications. Once you've said your piece, the ball is in your boss's court – so wait for their reply and take it from there.

Write it up

Whatever the outcome, make sure you get the agreement in writing. She who writes the minutes controls the conversation, so follow up with an email soon afterwards confirming everything that was agreed.

Set a goal

If your boss says no, query what you need to do to get a pay rise the next time you ask. Set a specific and realistic goal *together*, as well as a deadline to revisit the subject. And if the answer's still no? It's time to look for a new job.

NEGOTIATING A JOB OFFER

So you've just been offered your dream job – congrats! Given how tedious and protracted the job-hunting process can be, your initial inclination when you *finally* land a new job might very well be to jump at the first offer your potential employer makes – especially if you're currently stuck in a job you hate, or floating on a wave of bonhomie. Yet it's absolutely vital you negotiate hard at this stage, not least because all of your future salaries and pay rises within that organization will be pegged to your initial starting salary – so you want that figure to be as high as possible. Bear in mind too, that new job offer salaries are almost always at the bottom of the pay range for the role in question, as employers are *expecting* you to negotiate. Here are a few pointers on how to play your cards right:

Remember your advantage

Most employers don't particularly love the recruit-ment process – it's usually time-consuming, often boring and always expensive. If someone's made you a job offer, then they're probably hoping all of that is at an end, which is something you can and should use to your advantage. As their chosen 'ideal candidate', you actually hold a great deal of power at this stage, so, money-wise, go in for the kill.

Keep schtum

Try to sidestep being pinned to a salary too early on in the interview process, as you run the risk of either overpricing or underselling yourself. If pressed, give a broad range as opposed to a specific figure. If the interview process reveals that the job requires more from you than you initially thought, don't be afraid to revise that figure upwards when it comes up again – just be upfront about your reasons for doing so.

Play it cool

It'll probably feel incredibly counter-intuitive, but don't be *too* effusive or grateful in response to a new job offer, or say anything implying that you accepting the job is pretty much a done deal. If your would-be employer feels like you're probably going to accept the job come what may, then they've got *very* little incentive to improve on their offer. Keep your interactions pleasant, but neutral and non-committal.

Take your time
If you've been caught off-guard by an offer (i.e. if it's made over the phone or in person, as opposed to via email), don't feel pressured into responding to the salary on offer straight away. You're perfectly within your rights to ask for a little time to think it over, at which point you can gather your thoughts and build your case for a sweeter deal.

SETTING YOUR RATES
Particularly when quoting for bigger projects or commissions, you should always ask potential clients for their budget first, rather than quoting blind. Doing this will help you avoid misquoting so you don't come in wildly beyond their expectations, or lowball yourself and leave money on the table. If it seems like a client's fee really won't stretch to your rates but you're keen to make it work, instead of just slashing your rates try to see if there's room to negotiate on the deliverables (i.e. doing less work for them) – thereby still attaching the same level of value to your work.

REVIEWING YOUR RATES

If you're a freelancer, make sure you review your rates regularly. Have you recently been published in a few prestigious outlets, or worked for a well-known brand? Think about whether that affects your value and adjust your rates accordingly. You should be aiming for a steady increase over time. Don't be afraid to (politely) raise rates with regular clients too, although generally speaking don't do this more than once a year. Simply let them know that your rates will be going up for future jobs, and maybe offer to work one more project at your old rate to foster a bit of goodwill. If they refuse or are reluctant, consider slowly phasing them out over time and looking for clients who *are* willing to pay you what you're worth.

WORKING FOR FREE

An unfortunate reality of working in the creative industries is that, particularly when you're just starting out, you'll often be expected to work for free. Think of it as a (really crap) rite of passage. If the amount of money on offer for a project is 'none', make sure you're getting something tangible out of the deal that makes it worth your while, whether that's access, a referral, or a bigger platform. Don't be shy about asking for those things upfront either – don't assume they'll just magically come your way.

Still – rite of passage or not – a key part of knowing your worth comes down to always assigning at least a nominal value to your time and output. As you gain more experience, there'll probably still be a few rare occasions where the exposure, prestige, or contacts gained from a project can justify working for free or reduced rates, but, generally speaking, exposure doesn't pay the bills. Always ask to be paid, especially if you'd be devoting time to the project in question at the expense of *actual paid work*. The expectation of free labour within the creative industries is rampant, but try not to be flattered (or intimidated) into accepting unpaid work. Clients who claim to have 'no budget for this unfortunately' often can and will conjure up at least a small fee if you outright decline unpaid work. Sometimes it just takes a bit of negotiation. Be very wary of potential clients who tell you that an unpaid project 'will be good for your portfolio'. That's your decision, not theirs.

Chapter 6

MONEY TALKS PART II: TAKING CARE OF BUSINESS

MANAGING YOUR AFFAIRS

'My advice to women in general: even if you're doing a nine-to-five job, treat yourself like a boss. Not arrogant, but be sure of what you want.'
– Nicki Minaj, rapper

So payday's arrived, or that magazine you wrote for six months ago has *finally* processed your invoice – but how do you manage your money once you've got it? Glad you asked: welcome to Business 101.

BUDGETING

A simple rule for figuring out how much you should be spending, and on what, is the 50/30/20 rule. Essentially, no more than 50 per cent of your take-home income should go towards essentials such as rent, utilities, food and transportation. Aim to put at least 20 per cent of your income towards financial obligations such as pension contributions (yes, really), emergency savings, student loan repayments and general debt clearance. The final 30 per cent of your income is for the fun stuff: non-essentials such as new clothes, eating out and holidays.

You might need to tweak the proportions a little depending on your individual situation – sticking to the 50 per cent rule is obviously more difficult if, for instance, you live in an expensive city (hiya London), where rent alone takes up a more-than-ideal chunk of your salary. Overall, however, the 50/30/20 guideline is a good starting point for budgeting newbies.

PAY YOURSELF FIRST

How long would your savings last if you couldn't work, or lost your job? The answer should be at least three to six months. That means three to six months of being able to cover your rent, bills and day-to-day living expenses. Your spending priority before *anything* else should be making sure you have a comfortable financial cushion should things go wrong – what Paulette Perhach calls a 'fuck off fund'. When you get paid, transfer money into your savings account before doing anything else, or set up a monthly direct debit if that makes things easier. Think of this nest egg as your emergency parachute out of bad situations. Don't neglect it.

TRACKING SPENDING

In an increasingly cashless world, it can be difficult to keep track of your spending. Check your bank balance regularly even if it pains you to do so – in fact, check your bank balance regularly *especially* if it pains you to do so. Most banks offer to text you weekly updates so you know where you stand. Every few months, take fifteen minutes to scrutinize your bank transactions to get a clearer idea of what you're spending money on. Chances are you'll discover unexpected expenditures you hadn't factored in, and areas to cut back on. If you're Stateside, the Mint app is brilliant for tracking spending and creating budgets, while UK banking service Monzo is supported by an app that organizes all your bank transactions by category, making analysing your spending habits as easy as scrolling through Instagram.

FREELANCER FINANCES: TAXES

If you're self-employed, tax is a little bit more compli-cated than just sitting back and having your employer take care of everything. First up – get a decent accountant. It's money well spent, will save you time and generally just make your life a whole lot easier. A good accountant will also help you hang on to more of your income by advising on the most tax-efficient way of accounting for your earnings, whether that means incorporating as a company or reporting your income across different fiscal years.

Keeping track of tax owed on a monthly or quarterly basis and setting aside provisions accordingly will help you avoid getting caught short come tax season – if in doubt, over-save as opposed to under-save. That way if you have anything left over once you've paid your tax bill, you can treat yourself! Take fifteen minutes to set up an easy-access ISA to deposit your tax provision into, as money saved in ISAs is untaxed and can be interest-generating – so you can make your money go that little bit further before handing it over to the taxman. Some types of ISAs are riskier investments than others though, so make sure you consult an independent financial adviser and are fully clued-up before you stash your cash.

FREELANCER FINANCES: EXPENSES

If you're self-employed, many of the costs incurred in the running of your business (which technically is *you*) can be deducted from your total income to work out your taxable profit. Make sure you're clear on the various deductions, reliefs and allowances you're entitled to, as they're more extensive than people often realize. File your expenses once a month instead of leaving it until tax season to decipher a pile of tattered receipts; paid-for accounting software such as Xero, FreeAgent and Freshbooks are all great at helping you keep track of your income and expenditure. FreeAgent has the added benefit of allowing you to upload photos of receipts from your phone on the go, so you don't end up faffing around with endless bits of paper, or worse, forgetting to log your expenses altogether.

FREELANCER FINANCES: MANAGING YOUR CASH FLOW

Much like death and taxes, irregular cash flow is an unfortunate but inevitable fact of life for the self-employed. With that in mind, try to resist the urge to splurge after a big fee comes through, given that there might potentially be some leaner periods around the corner. Instead, pay yourself a set monthly salary, regardless of your fluctuating earnings. Building up a financial buffer so you're not dependent on one particular invoice – or beholden to one particular client – will allow you to make decisions about the kind of work you do from a place of security, not desperation. Regardless of whether you're set up as a sole trader or decide to incorporate as a company, having separate bank accounts for your business and personal expenditure will make managing your income far easier, and prove extremely handy when tax return season rolls around.

FREELANCER FINANCES: CONTRACTS AND SOWS

You should always get a written contract clearly outlining the terms of any project you're about to undertake, especially if you're working for a new client. It might seem overly formal, but having some kind of written agreement in place is vital for clarifying everyone's expectations, and protects *both* parties. As a starting point, your contract should spell out:

- The SOW (scope of work): outlining what is included as part of your fee, and what isn't.
- Details on how work that falls out of scope will be billed.

- A payment schedule: especially for larger projects and those where you might incur third-party costs on behalf of your client, being paid 33–50 per cent upfront is fairly standard practice.
- Details on who'll retain ownership of intellectual property rights for the work created, and a clear licensing agreement if relevant.
- Project timings and deadlines: be sure to include client feedback turnaround times too. You don't want a project being dragged out by a client who's slow to respond.

Always create a clear and itemized breakdown of the project's deliverables, so that your client understands exactly how their fee has been put together, as opposed to mentally assigning a lump sum to an overall project. Not only does that instil confidence in you, it also means that if something gets cut (or goes over), both parties know what proportion of the budget that affects. When it comes to putting a project scope together, transparency is key.

Depending on the type and scale of the project in question, you should also consider including a cancellation clause that makes provision for a 'kill fee' – so that if for some reason the project is cancelled after you've already started working on it, you still get at least partial compensation for your efforts. Ask around among creatives who do similar work so you're clear on what the standard terms are for your line of work – the kind of contract a writer might sign can be fairly different from that of a designer or illustrator.

FREELANCER FINANCES: INVOICING CLIENTS

You should have a clear and consistent invoicing system that keeps a record of the payment status of every job and tracks your invoices meticulously. It doesn't have to be anything fancy – a simple Excel spreadsheet will do the trick, and there are plenty of reliable templates freely available online. Keep a copy of every invoice you send or receive, and be sure to include the following details on all of your invoices:

- Your name/company name.
- Company number (if applicable).
- VAT number (if registered).
- Your registered office address.
- The word 'Invoice' on the document.
- A unique invoice number to help you keep track.

- The name and address of your client.
- The date, so you have proof of when the invoice was submitted.
- Item and description: briefly outline the service provided, and give a breakdown of time spent if your final fee is based on a day rate.
- Payment terms: include clear payment deadlines and a late payment clause that stipulates penalties for clients who fail to pay you on time.
- Payment details: make it clear how and to whom payments should be made. Include your bank's name, account number and sort code.
- Any relevant job/PO number issued by your client.
- Details of whoever commissioned you for reference, particularly if you're invoicing the accounts department of a large company.

FREELANCER FINANCES: DEALING WITH LATE PAYMENT

Set aside a weekly time slot to chase outstanding invoices, the bane of every freelancer's life. As well as including late payment clauses on your invoices (and enforcing them), another way of ensuring timely payment is to include terms on your contracts that specify intellectual property isn't transferred to your client until they've paid you in full. Essentially, this means that the work you've done isn't theirs to use until they've paid you, which gives you greater leverage and can be particularly useful if you've been commissioned to create work where ownership of the intellectual property in question is important.

PROTECTING YOUR WORK

If you work in a creative field, it's crucial you have at least a basic understanding of intellectual property rights – mostly for the sake of protecting your own work, but also to ensure you don't unintentionally land yourself in a sticky situation by infringing on that of others. While social media and the Internet have made it easier than ever to share your work publicly, they also make it far easier for you to lose track of it – and for other people to help themselves to the fruits of your labour. As a creative, your ideas and output are your greatest assets, so it's vital you take the necessary measures to avoid being exploited, misled, or just outright ripped off.

KNOW YOUR RIGHTS

While trademarks and copyrights both provide protection for intellectual property, they do so in fairly different ways. Trademarks generally cover names, taglines, logos, or any other unique entity that might distinguish your brand from that of another company. Copyrights protect original creative works (e.g. written work, music, photographs, etc.) and give the creator of the work in question the right to determine how and by whom their work is used by other people, if at all.

STAKE YOUR CLAIM

If you've decided to set up a brand or business, your very first step should be to register your brand name and/or logo as a trademark. By registering a trademark with the Intellectual Property Office (UK), European Union Intellectual Property Office (EU), or the United States Patent and Trademark Office (USA), you're effectively documenting your ownership of the entity in question under the law – meaning that if someone *does* rip you off or infringe on your trademark, it's far easier to defend your right to it. It's also worth making ownership of any work you create crystal clear by marking it with the copyright symbol ©, your name and the year of creation – what's known as a copyright notice. While the UK doesn't have a formal copyright register, if you're US-based you can formally copyright your work via the US Copyright Office, which gives you an added layer of legal protection in the event of someone trying to copy or steal your work (although your work will still be under copyright even without this formal registration).

GET A CONTRACT

When it comes to protecting your rights, having a contract that clearly outlines the terms under which you're operating is crucial. Clauses to look out for include:

Work for hire

IP (intellectual property) can be a hugely valuable asset, and while you should generally endeavour to retain rights to the work you produce, it's also very common for creatives to be asked to produce 'work for hire' (i.e. work where your client will automatically own the IP in question). Common though it may be, if clients are asking you to sign over ownership of the work you create, as opposed to merely licensing it from you, you're perfectly within your rights to use that as a bargaining chip to charge them more. Either way, any contract you sign should always clearly specify who's going to retain ownership of intellectual property rights over the completed work.

Indemnity clauses

While indemnity clauses are fairly standard practice, be sure to check they're not overly broad or punitive in scope.

Work product

Is the work you generate along the way yours to keep once the project has concluded? For example, if you create six concepts for an eventual final selection of one, are the other five ideas you developed along the way yours to repurpose as you like (e.g. for a future client), or does your client retain ownership of those as well? Get clear on this upfront to avoid any unpleasant surprises further down the line.

Similarly if you're a company employee, usually the IP for work you create automatically belongs to your employer. When signing an employee contract, be extremely clear on what it means for your ability to use, monetize or share the work you create while under contract once you've left the company in question. Particularly if you're a content creator or working within media, think carefully about whether the trade-off of a bigger platform and better resources in exchange for ownership of your creative ideas is one you're happy making.

If you're feeling unsure about an intellectual property issue or the terms of a contract, your best bet is to get professional help and talk to an IP lawyer. Some of the most costly legal battles within business are fought over the ownership of intellectual property (Louboutin vs YSL anyone?), and even if you feel like you're too small-time to have to think about this, you never know how big your ideas will become. The effects of decisions regarding intellectual property can be far-reaching and come into play in unexpected ways long after you've made them, so get protected. If you're UK-based, the Institute of Trademark Attorneys (ITMA) offers free resources and legal advice clinics for anyone grappling with the process of registering a trademark, as does the British Library Business & IP Centre.

GETTING AN AGENT

From landing you more prestigious gigs to boosting your profile, as a creative getting an agent can very often help take your career to the next level. At its most basic, an agent's role is to help you manage the financial and commercial aspects of your work – negotiating contracts and fees on your behalf, and ensuring you're fairly compensated for your work. In general, having an agent will probably also help you get *more* work, as they'll likely have a network of industry contacts and insider knowledge that can lead to opportunities you'd probably find hard to come by on your own. The very best agents may well be instrumental in helping you develop your talent and career, pointing you in the direction of good opportunities and steering you away from the bad. If you're in the market for an agent, make sure you shop around and meet a couple of different people before committing to a particular person or agency, so you have a decent frame of reference. More so than most, this is a working relationship that relies on a good personality fit – you should feel that the person you sign with has a clear and instinctive understanding of your work, your goals and your tastes.

Chapter 7

BACK TO SCHOOL

HOW AND WHY TO LEARN NEW SKILLS

'You must feed your mind with reading material, thoughts, and ideas that open you to new possibilities.'
– Oprah Winfrey, media mogul

Learning new skills doesn't have to stop once you've left school or university. In an ideal world, your chosen career and workplace will be environments in which you're constantly developing and learning new things, but sometimes more structured learning can be beneficial, too. Whether you've got something in particular in mind, or just want a bit of inspiration, here's the how, the why and the where.

WHY DO IT?

Adding an extra string to your bow makes you more employable and can seriously improve your salary prospects. When your creative output is also your source of income, it can be easy to limit yourself to a specific field – the one that pays the bills. Yet experimenting with new ideas can give you fresh perspectives that actually enhance your main craft, as discussed in Chapter 2.

Being self-sufficient

Picking up new skills can save you money in the long run: taking a basic Photoshop or InDesign course, for example, means you can do basic design work yourself instead of paying someone else to do it for you.

Health benefits

Learning new things keeps your brain sharp, and actually makes it easier for your brain to pick up new concepts and skills in the future. Plus, there's the sense of achievement you'll get from stepping out of your comfort zone and pushing yourself a little.

Career clarity

Learning a new skill can give you a clearer sense of professional purpose by exposing you to areas you hadn't considered before – it's not unusual for adult learning classes to prompt career changes. If you're curious about an area, dipping your toe in the pool via a short course is a great way of giving it a test run. You never know when your newly acquired knowledge will open new doors.

HOW TO DO IT

Two of the biggest challenges are – predictably – finding the time and money to dedicate to further learning. Most educational organizations have distance learning and online options you can complete at times that are convenient for you, if your job isn't flexible enough to accommodate attending daytime courses. Although they won't necessarily advertise it, lots of employers also offer partial or full funding for employee training and development. Check in with your HR department to see what's on offer and whether they can foot the bill. If you're UK-based, your local authority usually offers a range of low-cost adult education courses, with the added bonus of them being right on your doorstep. If you're learning as part of a group, chances are everyone else will be in exactly the same boat and feeling just as nervous – so don't be afraid to ask lots of questions and get your money's worth.

WHERE TO DO IT

Everyone's optimal learning style is different – some people prefer to dive straight in on their own and figure things out through trial and error, while others thrive in a more structured learning environment. If you want a bit more guidance, here's a round-up of some of the best adult education resources around.

General Assembly

GA bills itself as a 'global education network for entrepreneurs' and offers educational courses in tech, business, design and marketing, with a strong focus on job placement. They have campuses in many major cities worldwide, and their range of scheduling options – full vs part-time, online vs on-site – mean whether you work nine to five or have a more flexible schedule, there'll be something that works for you. While their longer term and on-site courses can be a little pricey, they also have online workshops and short classes that start from as little as £15/$20.

Skillshare

An online learning platform that offers classes taught by fellow creatives, Skillshare's classes can be enjoyed at your own pace, from the comfort of your own home. With classes ranging from design to SEO skills, you can either choose from a host of free classes, learn on a pay-as-you-go basis, or sign up for a monthly subscription that allows you unlimited access. Classes are bite-size – generally thirty minutes or less – meaning you can pick up a new skill in the amount of time it takes to do your morning commute.

Duolingo
A fun language-learning app, Duolingo's bite-sized lessons are a great way to pick up a second language, or at the very least pick up a few key phrases for your next holiday destination.

Lynda
Much like Skillshare, Lynda offers an exhaustive range of free and paid online classes taught by experts within their field, covering a variety of business, tech and creative skills. It's particularly good if you want to get to grips with updates on software such as Photoshop or InDesign, as they offer 'tune-up' classes for new versions of most software programs.

City Lit London
One of London's leading destinations for adult education, City Lit offers a class on virtually every subject under the sun and generally receives glowing reviews

from former students. Many of the courses take place in the evenings or weekends and they have plenty of one-off sessions too, so you can still fit them in around your nine to five. Signing up for a course also gives you access to their modern building and café, so there's the bonus of a well-equipped central London workspace.

Brit & Co
Though online creativity hub Brit & Co is more focused on craft and DIY classes for those looking for more hands-on skills, it also breaks down topics such as the basics of coding or web page design in a straightforward, easy-to-use manner.

Chapter 8

THE ART OF NETWORKING

BECAUSE WHO YOU KNOW IS AS IMPORTANT AS WHAT YOU KNOW

'Never doubt that a small group of thoughtful committed citizens can change the world. Indeed, it is the only thing that ever has.'
– Margaret Mead, cultural anthropologist

Networking tends to get a bad rep, with many people thinking it consists solely of stuffy corporate events and business card-toting suits. For every natural-born networker there's another person standing nearby who'd rather drink cold paint than 'work the room'. But, love it or loathe it, the art of successful networking is a skill worth mastering, whether you're just starting out or a bit more established. The adage 'it's not what you know, it's who you know' hasn't become a cliché without good reason, and people you know are very often the best sources of new opportunities. Read on for the 411 on graceful networking.

NETWORK IN ALL DIRECTIONS

It's all very well and good pitching the power players in your industry, but chances are they're pretty busy, and you'll also be competing with a *lot* of other people for their time. Peer-to-peer networking (i.e. meeting people who are at similar points in their careers to you) is equally as important – it can be just as helpful to bounce ideas off your peers as someone more senior, so don't neglect the networking opportunities more readily available to you. Plus, your career and those of your peers will probably progress in tandem, so the relationships you build now could be even more helpful further down the line. Effective networking is all about playing the long game.

BE RECIPROCAL

The best networkers are genuinely interested in other people's projects and problems, and not just what they can get out of a given situation. Be known as someone who offers to help others out as well as asking for things, and make an effort to nurture professional relationships on an ongoing basis – not just when you need something. Be a connector: if you have mutual contacts you think might benefit from knowing each other, introduce them. Not only are people more likely to engage with you if they see your relationship as being mutually beneficial, it's also just good karma!

START SMALL

Whether you're at an industry event or a one-on-one meeting, don't just launch straight into your elevator pitch when striking up a conversation with people. This is one scenario where small talk is good talk. When you *do* get down to work chat, ask about people's current projects. Most people tend to light up given a chance to talk about what they're working on at the moment, and asking about that as opposed to just interrogating them about their job title gives the conversation more chance to develop. You've probably heard about good conversationalists asking open-ended questions, and this is just an extension of that principle.

ANYTIME, ANYPLACE

Be open-minded about where you might meet interesting professional contacts. Networking doesn't have to be limited to specialist industry events. You're just as likely to meet interesting people in social situations, and through friends.

COLD EMAILING

Getting that all-important face-time often starts out with an email, which means sending a missive into an already overflowing inbox. So how can you make your email stand out?

Signpost
Make the purpose of your email clear from the outset. A punchy subject line could be the difference between someone opening your email and sending it straight to Trash, so make sure it doesn't sound spammy or generic. Don't hide your light under a bushel either – if you've got something compelling to say that you think is likely to elicit a response, don't save it for the last line of your email. Signpost that in the subject of the email, too.

Keep it concise
Your initial email shouldn't be more than a few sentences – don't write an essay, because it won't be read. If the person you're contacting wants more information, you can follow up with that if and when they reply, and are more engaged.

Get personal
Outline why you're getting in touch with them in particular. People can smell a template mass email a mile off, and they won't respond – personalize your email so it's directly relevant to them or their work.

Have a clear ask
The recipient of your email should be left with a clear question, so avoid generic phrases like 'pick your brain' (even if that's what you want). Don't make them have to work to figure out what you want – make it as easy as possible for them to say 'yes' by hanging the structure of your email around one or two clear asks. Doing this will also force you to get clear on exactly what it is you want out of the interaction.

Persist
Don't be afraid to follow up with people if you don't get a response, although give it a week or so before you chase. Having said that, don't badger people with emails – two follow-ups is probably the limit before you start to become a pest, so if they haven't replied by that point it's probably time to call it quits.

CONNECT IRL

Emails are great for making initial contact, but nothing beats the power of a face-to-face meeting. A half-hour coffee date is a hundred times more powerful than dozens of emails, so when you're reaching out cold to someone, meeting them in person should be your go-to goal for all but the most cursory of relationships. Always gun for that if you think it's an option; people are more likely to remember or help out people they feel they know, and you can't get to know an email address. Once you've got that all-important face-time scheduled, here's how to get the most out of it.

Be on time
This one doesn't really need explaining.

Do your research
Don't turn up armed with questions that a cursory Google could have revealed the answer to. It's lazy, and a waste of both your time.

Have a clear ask (again)
As with an email, you should have a clear ask or goal in mind for the meeting. If you're the one who

initiated the meeting, be prepared to steer the conversation. Don't make your contact do the work.

Wrap up on time
Don't make your contact late for their next meeting. Keep an eye on the clock and stick to the amount of time agreed, unless they say they're happy to stay for longer.

Get a referral
A great way of ending a meeting is by asking your contact if there's anyone who they think you should meet, thereby potentially getting an introduction to someone who might be of interest. It's a great way to expand your network, and people are often only too happy to play the role of 'connector'.

Follow up
Send an email thanking them for their time within a day or two, while you're still fresh on their mind – this is also a good opportunity to remind them of anything they agreed to do or send, and for you to do likewise.

Chapter 9

LOOKING AFTER NUMBER ONE

KEEPING YOUR MIND AND BODY ON TRACK

'If you don't take control over your time and your life, other people will gobble it up.'
– Michelle Obama, lawyer and former FLOTUS

You're probably already well aware of how essential taking care of your mental, physical and emotional wellbeing is to your ability to work productively and efficiently – and yet, somehow, when things are busy on the work front, self-care is very often the first thing to take a back seat. It's incredibly easy to forget, but prioritizing work at the expense of your health is the ultimate false economy. Being consistently stressed out, overworked, or run down is a terrible starting point from which to produce good work. Practising self-care is as vital to your career as turning up to work every day, so here are some straightforward ideas to help you do just that.

MIND

Prevention is always better than cure, and identifying a few go-to stress management techniques *before* your stress levels spiral out of control is the best way of making sure they don't. One tried and tested method that's great for creative thinkers is mindfulness, a form of meditation stemming from early Buddhist practice. With benefits that include improving your focus and boosting your memory, it's a useful technique for busy creatives juggling lots of different commitments. Here's how to incorporate mindfulness into your daily routine.

Mornings
When you first wake up in the morning, spend two minutes in bed with your eyes closed, simply focusing on the movement of your breath flowing in and out of your body. Whenever you feel your mind drifting towards distracting thoughts about the day ahead, bring your focus back to the sensation of your breath entering and leaving your body.

At work

Once you arrive at work, take a few minutes at your desk to do the same breathing exercise, to centre yourself before getting down to business. Repeat as necessary throughout the day whenever you feel things getting a bit overwhelming.

Home time

Tempting as it is to while away your commute glued to your phone, spend at least some of it with your music off and phone stowed away in your bag, just focusing on your breathing.

Bedtime

Once you're tucked up in bed, spend two minutes replicating your morning wake-up routine, this time visualizing all the thoughts and worries of the day literally melting away.

Don't overwhelm yourself by trying to adopt these exercises all at once. Keep things manageable by picking one or two occasions where you think you'd benefit most from a greater sense of calm, and start with those. The waking up/bedtime combo, practised from the comfort of your own bed, is a good place to start. The exercises will soon become second nature, and you can build up from there.

BODY

When it comes to creativity, the physical informs the mental. Giving your body the TLC it deserves will set you up to do your best work, and keep your ideas flowing. Here's how.

Food for thought

Around 20 to 30 per cent of your daily calorie intake is used to regulate your brain function, so if you're not well fed you'll have trouble operating at full force. The key to maintaining a healthy diet even when you're under pressure is to plan ahead – when you're pressed for time, it's far too easy to reach for unhealthy ready meals, or even skip meals altogether. Why not try preparing larger batches of food in advance at the weekends, to save yourself time and energy during the week? If you work from home, try to accumulate a go-to repertoire of a few speedy lunch options. Make sure you've also got the right kind of snacks to hand to keep you going between meals. Low-GI foods like nuts, (unsweetened) popcorn, carrots topped with hummus or guacamole, and dark chocolate are all 'brain foods', so they'll stave off hunger pangs *and* boost your brainpower. Win-win.

Keep it moving

Making time for regular exercise is a hugely important aspect of your self-care regime – the endorphin rush from a great workout can lift even the sourest of moods, and letting your thoughts drift is a great way of getting your creative juices flowing. Ideally, you should aim to work out around two to three times a week, and the key to making exercise a regular part of your everyday life is finding an activity you genuinely enjoy. Just because everyone you know seems to be an avid runner or SoulCycle addict, doesn't necessarily mean that'll work for you, so experiment until you find something that does – whether that's a lung-busting cardio class, a chilled-out yoga session or something in between. Working out doesn't have to be expensive either – skip the pricey gym membership and try a free app or YouTube fitness channel for luxe personal trainer vibes in the comfort of your own home. FitnessBlender and the Nike+ Training Club app are both great places to start.

Catch some zzz's

Getting enough shut-eye is vital for staying on top of your game, and the quality of sleep you get is just as important as the quantity. If either one of those is off-kilter, then your daytime energy and productivity levels will bear the brunt. Try to set aside half an hour before bed to wind down with a book, or whatever it is that helps your brain slow down after a hectic day. This wind-down period should also be a totally screen-free zone, as exposure to blue light immediately before bed significantly affects your sleep quality by preventing your body from releasing the chemical that helps you sleep. Be sure to put your phone on silent before bed, and leave it outside your bedroom along with your laptop. Your bed should be a source of sanity not stress, which means making it a work-free zone – no answering emails or doing a quick bit of online banking in bed, OK?

BALANCE

When it comes to the creative industries, the lines between the personal and the professional are often pretty blurry, and drawing a clear distinction between work and home can be difficult – especially if you're self-employed and actually work *from* home. Read on for some pointers on how to find that ever-elusive work-life balance.

Establish some boundaries

Carving out some personal space outside of the work you do is crucial to maintaining a sense of self. Think consciously about where you want to draw the line between the personal and the professional, and create a few rules that help you do that. They could be anything from not replying to emails in the evenings or at weekends, to keeping your Facebook friend list a work-free zone. Whatever they are, once you've put these boundaries in place it's up to you to respect them, thereby sending the message to other people that they're not up for negotiation.

Know your limits

While constantly challenging yourself is important for your professional growth, be mindful of biting off more than you can chew. Always consider new requests in the context of existing commitments and deadlines. Particularly if you're self-employed, it's often better to say no and maintain a good relationship with a potential client or employer as opposed to delivering work that's rushed or half-assed, and risk damaging the relationship for good. Remember: there'll be a next time.

Stay social

Human beings are social creatures – we need regular social interaction to stay happy and sane, so be sure to schedule in regular down time with friends to stop yourself from getting into a funk. If you're a freelancer and usually work solo, team up with a fellow freelance friend and pick one day a week to work together. Creative work is very often a solitary endeavour, but that doesn't mean you have to go through it alone.

Treat yourself

Don't forget to reward yourself for a job well done! An afternoon with a stack of fresh magazines, a cute manicure, a relaxing weekend away . . . whatever floats your boat. Never underestimate the power of some straight-up indulgence to boost your spirits and rejuvenate the soul.

Say 'no' more often

The word 'no' is one of the most powerful tools in your arsenal when it comes to protecting your time and energy. Not all requests or opportunities are created equal, and stretching yourself too thin in an attempt to accommodate every request that comes your way is a sure-fire way to make everyone happy except yourself – and that's *if* you manage to fulfil all of your obligations. Whenever your inner people-pleaser gives you a hard time over saying no to someone, or you're tempted to say yes to something because you feel too awkward about the alternative, try to remind yourself of what's really on the line. The opportunity cost of saying 'yes' when you really ought to say 'no' is time that could be spent doing other more fruitful work (or y'know, relaxing). Weighing up what you're sacrificing in order to make room for superfluous requests can be pretty damn motivating.

Chapter 10

Q&A

WORDS OF WISDOM FROM SOME INSPIRATIONAL WOMEN

'Because you deserve better than made-up
Marilyn Monroe quotes.'
– Otegha Uwagba, founder of Women Who

WHAT ADVICE WOULD YOU GIVE TO OTHER WORKING WOMEN?

Know your worth and assert it. Women are still
vilified for exercising the tenacity and assertiveness
that men are applauded for in work situations, and
that's magnified in creative industries, where you
see young women putting in huge emotional
investments yet still feeling like they need to
downplay their abilities. Which is bullshit. You have
to become your own biggest cheerleader, even if it
makes you cringe at first.

Jo Fuertes-Knight, journalist

Apologize only when you've done something that actually requires apology. Don't apologize for speaking your mind or saying no or claiming your space or having ambition or taking credit when it is your due.

Chimamanda Ngozi Adichie, writer

I do think it's important to be unapologetic about what you do. I used to mumble aspects of my job – flagging up only the bits I thought sounded most mainstream – but now I try hard to give each thing I do the weight it deserves.

Pandora Sykes, journalist and stylist

Take up space – don't be apologetic about your ideas and opinions. Men aren't.

Linsey Young, curator at Tate Britain

The one thing you really need to know before starting a business is yourself. You need to know your limits, and how far you're willing to go. You're going to have to work really hard – do you have that in you? Is this something you're really passionate about? What are your strengths, and what can hold you back?

Serena Guen, founder and CEO of *SUITCASE Magazine*

I think my answer to this question has changed a lot since having a baby. Before, I'd have said something about being assertive and making use of the unique position you have in the fashion world, by being both the creative and the target market. But now I realize the challenges that women face are not only external obstacles, but internal ones as well. I now have to be successful and work to the detriment of my relationship with my baby, and that is a sacrifice that I have to feel good about – but I reason that I now work harder when I'm at work because of what I have given up to be there. I need to make every second in my studio count, and I feel like that is really helping to focus my work, and take me into a new chapter of my career.

Quentin Jones, illustrator and filmmaker

Be true to yourself. Creative living requires you to be vulnerable, emotionally honest, and open to both your intuition and the world around you. I think that the most important advice is to follow your intuition and stay true to your values above all else. I've found that the most fulfillment comes when my soul is my goal path.

Piera Gelardi, executive creative director and co-founder at Refinery29

Don't keep your ideas to yourself. Be confident that you can do it better than the next person, but for that to happen your idea needs to be out there so people can feed back on it, and help you get what and where you need. I've found that people are very eager to give time to someone who is passionate about something.

Lana Elie, founder and CEO of Floom

To assume gender equality at all times, even when evidence of the opposite is staring you in the face, and doggedly proceed under that assumption.

Penny Martin, editor-in-chief of *The Gentlewoman*

Trust your instincts, because they're always right. Also – no matter what – remember to carve out alone time to reflect and regroup, because you'll never be as productive as you can be if you don't. It's easy to feel that you should be working all the time, but down time is equally important.

Victoria Spratt, journalist

One thing I've found really useful is sticking to the 20 per cent rule (or at least that's what I call it). The next time you negotiate a salary or payment, ask for 20 per cent more than you think you deserve –

because you've almost certainly been undervalued, whether unconsciously by yourself, or by the people paying you. So just go for that extra 20 per cent. Maybe your employers go for it, maybe they won't – but you'll definitely feel better for having tried. And when you've tried it once, that makes it easier to do it again.

Zing Tsjeng, journalist and Broadly editor

Get help. I spent a long time believing I had to do it all, and that no one else would do the job as well as me. That's bullshit. Sure, no one can write my books for me, but getting help with the other stuff means I can free up my brain for the deep work that I really love.

Anna Jones, cook, stylist and writer

Be in this together. Be with each other. Respect all industries and the work they entail, even if you don't understand them. Collaborate – cross-pollinate each other with your skills and experiences. Make friends.

Missy Flynn, restaurateur

Always pick up the phone over sending an email. And always eat breakfast.

Alicia Lawson, director of Rubies in the Rubble

Be enthusiastic and amicable, but don't let anyone walk over you. Get in touch with everyone you want to work for and make sure they know who you are.

Francesca Allen, photographer

Really get to know your industry inside and out, not just your own specific role. I meet so many people who say they want to (for example) be a fashion editor – but if that's what you want to do, then you really should know how a buyer's job works, how a designer's job works . . . heck even how the intern's job works! All of those things affect you. Also – don't be afraid to take risks. Sure they might not always work out exactly how you planned, but better to have tried.

Lynette Nylander, writer, editor and creative consultant

Guilt about what you haven't done or can't achieve makes a louder noise in your head than joy at what you have done, and have achieved. Be mindful of your own expectations of yourself and remember to celebrate your creativity, your problem solving and your sheer can-do attitude at the end of each day. If you are appreciative of yourself, so will others be.

Caryn Franklin MBE,
fashion commentator and agent of change

That boardrooms are places you should exist in. That doing something you care about will mean you do a better job. That eight hours of sleep a night is necessary. Ask more questions. Take more baths. Your work-life balance will constantly hang in the balance, but ultimately you decide which way the scales tip. Be aware of the times when work has to come first, and sensitive to those moments when your family and friends should be your priority. Don't compare yourself to anyone. Be focused. Go slower. Be a perfectionist, even if it doesn't come naturally.

Nellie Eden, co-founder of Babyface

HOW DO YOU MAINTAIN A HEALTHY WORK-LIFE BALANCE?

I followed a career in a field I might have chosen as a hobby so there can be confusion between what constitutes work and leisure. But I have learned to enjoy humdrum things, and I think that's the trick: you have to choose whether your professional or your personal life is going to be the high-octane one, and make sure the other is more low-key and restorative.

Penny Martin, editor-in-chief of _The Gentlewoman_

I maintain a healthy work life balance by not being afraid to let my job overlap with my life. I come from an artistic, entrepreneurial family. They are my biggest inspiration. Growing up in a family business taught me that work was part of life, and that it could be a source of energy, not a draining bore. Those borders were always blurred. Today, I work with several of my dearest friends, as well as my husband, and having a familial feel in the office is something that I love, and part of what makes R29 such a joyful place to work for me. To me, it's important to have gratitude and recognize the many amazing opportunities and people that surround me. I also really believe in carving out space for myself daily, whether that's listening to an inspiring podcast on my commute, taking small vacations tacked on to work trips, or simply taking the time to make breakfast in the morning. If you're go go go all the time, it's hard to have perspective.

Piera Gelardi, executive creative director and co-founder at Refinery29

When I get home after a day in the studio, I leave my phone downstairs and give my son a bath and put him to bed without interruption. When he was first born I was trying to do emails while taking care of him, and I wasn't doing well at either job. The same goes for holidays – I've stopped taking my laptop so I don't feel tempted to open it up and play with work files. Being a freelance creative, it's easy to allow whatever your current project is to take over all aspects of your life – but actually when you look back on the important moments of the last five years, you won't remember that online film or whatever it was that seemed so important to you at the time.

Quentin Jones, illustrator and filmmaker

I work out three or four times a week, and it makes me feel so much better. You need to do something that makes you not think about work for a bit, and exercise really helps. If you don't spend time away from work you'll never get the perspective you need to make really good decisions.

Serena Guen, founder and CEO of *SUITCASE Magazine*

I try to have one day at the weekend that's a phone-free zone. It's important to be connected but it's equally important to be present in the moment, and remember that you're no good to anyone if you're spread too thin and trying to do a zillion things at once.

Victoria Spratt, journalist

A constant battle for us all, I've learned to manage myself not as an inexhaustible resource but as a finely tuned being, and to say 'I'm sorry but I can't fit that in this week'. There is the temptation to think that because we have been asked, that we are therefore the only person who can do something. Not true. I let some projects or opportunities go in the knowledge that I am not a cog in a wheel, but a creative who needs space. Relationships with loved ones have also helped enormously to remind me of the importance of being, rather than doing.

Caryn Franklin MBE,
fashion commentator and agent of change

Evenings and weekends are sacrosanct – I keep them completely work-free. I could – and have – worked every hour available, and it's possible to do that and still produce great work, but it's at the cost of the rest of your life. Having my little boy has been the best perspective check I've had.

Anna Jones, cook, stylist and writer

Time blocking helps me differentiate when I'm on the clock, and when I'm 'off' – I only just learned how to do that. Also, there is no such thing as 'no time' when it comes to self-care. You have to make the time, because your happiness radiates from you, to clients and employees alike. Finally: defer replying to one email a day and, instead, use that time to write a few lines to a friend. Friendships are something that can really take a hit when work becomes your number one, but business is lonely, and even more so when you let the people who really know and love you slip away.

Missy Flynn, restaurateur

I've always made sure I have friends who do things outside of fashion. They don't care about the new collections or about a designer leaving a house and I need that! I couldn't and wouldn't be well rounded without having all the wine-filled dinners about politics, culture and our personal lives that we do. As much as working and achieving your goals is an amazing and gratifying feeling, work is just one facet of this big bowl of confusion we call life, and you need to have joys and pleasures outside of it. Cultivate a hobby to occupy your mind when you're not at work, and remember to enjoy life in and out of the office.

Lynette Nylander, writer, editor and creative consultant

I focus quite narrowly on what really matters to me and how I want to spend my time.

Chimamanda Ngozi Adichie, writer

My new thing since going freelance, is to take a walk each day and call a friend.

Pandora Sykes, journalist and stylist

By sticking to social plans made in advance, so I have to leave the office at a reasonable hour.

Alicia Lawson, director of Rubies in the Rubble

Nothing is ever that deep that you can't turn your phone off for a couple of hours. The end.

Jo Fuertes-Knight, journalist

WHAT DAY-TO-DAY ESSENTIALS DO YOU RELY ON?

Yoga and breathing to a musical soundtrack of birds and waterfalls first thing; clothes that make me feel great because I'm comfortable and I look the part; a power perfume (currently Portrait of a Lady by Frédéric Malle); and a hard-copy diary and notebook because I love writing things down, making lists and crossing things off – not to mention doodling when I'm on the phone. I stretch my body or move it when I can. I play music – fast for a deadline and slow for creativity. Oh, and when I'm working from home I talk to myself . . . a lot.

Caryn Franklin MBE,
fashion commentator and agent of change

Yoga, or some form of exercise. An alarm clock radio, not the alarm on my phone. Mascara. An actual calculator. Kiehl's Cactus Flower Hydrating Mist, for when I'm stuck inside but want to freshen up and feel close to nature.

Missy Flynn, restaurateur

A creative sounding board. I have a handful of people I use as a sounding board for big decisions. They include a film producer (who happens to be my sister), another cook, a writer and my husband. They are people who know me inside out, and have no interests in my business – but they love and know me well enough to tell me the (sometimes ugly) truth.

Anna Jones, cook, stylist and writer

Coffee and a tight deadline.

Francesca Allen, photographer

My day-to-day essentials are a morning cup of coffee, making breakfast at home, and getting in a good workout at least 3 days a week. I also rely on laughter and the power of bringing play into my every day – the best brainstorms are accompanied by fits of hysterical giggles. I really believe in the magic of humour and openness in the creative process.

**Piera Gelardi, executive creative director
and co-founder at Refinery29**

Lip balm. The voices and wisdom and love of my family and friends.

Chimamanda Ngozi Adichie, writer

A huge Mac desktop (my luxury), chewing gum, my Bailey and Nelson glasses and, if possible, an oily bath every single day – if only for 5 minutes.

Pandora Sykes, journalist and stylist

Reading and radio for mental rest; postcard writing to inject a bit of random altruism into a work-oriented day; taxi travel when my schedule gets a bit overloaded and I need a break; television for escapism; diary writing to stay in touch with my inner dialogue.

Penny Martin, editor-in-chief of *The Gentlewoman*

Sleep. Seriously. I want to say something romantic and tangible like a notebook containing my thoughts and feelings, but I'd be lying. There is nothing heroic or productive about depriving yourself of valuable bedtime.

Jo Fuertes-Knight, journalist

A clean and tidy wardrobe, so it's easy for me to choose what to wear in the morning. A nice fragrance, because smelling good puts me in a good mood. My glasses, because I can't really see shit without them, especially when I'm working. And a good candle for when I get back home in the evening – Cire Trudon make my favourites.

Lynette Nylander, writer, editor and creative consultant

Fast broadband and a good ol'-fashioned notepad.

Alicia Lawson, director of Rubies in the Rubble

My phone, Google Calendar and the Adobe Creative programs. I also need a cup of coffee each morning (followed by every type of tea throughout the day), a scalpel, black ink pens, my bike to get around and yoga classes a few times a week to balance things out.

Quentin Jones, illustrator and filmmaker

Elizabeth Arden. Good books. A Muji 0.38 navy pen. A Moleskine. Coffee. Coconut oil.

Nellie Eden, co-founder of Babyface

WHAT MAXIMS DO YOU LIVE OR WORK BY?

Don't drink the pickle juice. There's an interview with Nicki Minaj where she talks about being 'bossed up' and standing up for herself, saying: 'If I had accepted the pickle juice, I would be drinking pickle juice right now.' An old colleague and I turned that into our mantra. Every time we went into a meeting where we knew people were going to try to walk all over us, we'd whisper, 'don't drink the pickle juice' to each other. Personally, I found it very helpful.

Zing Tsjeng, journalist and Broadly editor

Nobody died. My mum's an NHS nurse so any time I call her with work-related histrionics she's like, 'Okay, but did anyone die?' That looks awful written down, but it's been a surprisingly effective mantra for forcing me to be pragmatic and solution-driven with my work.

Jo Fuertes-Knight, journalist

Go big or go home! Only in terms of work, though – I'm in bed by ten every night.

Linsey Young, curator at Tate Britain

Don't work for free, and don't sell out without getting paid. Don't take crap from anyone, and don't let people make you feel bad or awkward.

Francesca Allen, photographer

If you don't ask you don't get. Most of the breaks I've had in my career have come from contacting people I respect to tell them how much I rate them, and asking if there are any opportunities to learn from them.

Anna Jones, cook, stylist and writer

Question everything.

Serena Guen, founder and CEO of *SUITCASE Magazine*

Work hard, play hard. My dad told me that was how he lived when I was a teenager, and from then on I've tried to follow in his path.

Quentin Jones, illustrator and filmmaker

You're only as good as your team.

Missy Flynn, restaurateur

I really like the idea of being the one to make the change. So, if it's not the normal way to do things, then be the one to change it up. Anything done well is legitimised by its success.

Pandora Sykes, journalist and stylist

What is for you, won't go by you.

Lynette Nylander, writer, editor and creative consultant

Spread the joy and be open to joy. I like people, and I try to get the best out of them by being as warm and supportive as I can – but I've learned the hard way that I'm not superwoman, and that I can't be all things to all people or save a situation when it's broken. I've stopped suppressing my inner voice, which for the most part is trying to help me by saying what needs to be said. I'm still learning to say what needs to be said with grace and humility, which is really hard when I feel very challenged, but I feel there is better progress when there is a higher level of emotional exchange.

**Caryn Franklin MBE,
fashion commentator and agent of change**

Ask, ask, and ask again.

Lana Elie, founder and CEO of Floom

My motto is 'forever forward' which is all about always moving forward, forgiving yourself for mistakes, and being a proud work in progress . . . recognising that you have to put in the work in order to progress.

Piera Gelardi, executive creative director and co-founder at Refinery29

If you talk about doing something three times – do it.

Nellie Eden, co-founder of Babyface

Never admire quietly. Never disapprove quietly. Above all else, be true.

Chimamanda Ngozi Adichie, writer

EVERYDAY RESOURCES

THINGS TO READ

The Artist's Way | Julia Cameron
Originator of the morning pages ritual, this long-time classic on unlocking your creativity at times comes across as a little 'out there', but put your cynicism aside because, to be blunt, it works.

Fail Better | Zadie Smith
What makes a good writer? Words from one of the best.

Getting to Yes | Roger Fisher
A guide to negotiating, this best-selling classic offers simple but effective advice that can be applied to every aspect of your working life.

How to Find Fulfilling Work | **Roman Krznaric**
The School of Life book series is packed with good ideas for everyday living, and this is a particular high-light, full of practical thought exercises to help you get closer to a career you enjoy. You'll return to it time and time again.

Proposals for the Feminine Economy | **Jennifer Armbrust**
Business adviser Armbrust's thought-provoking model of how we can build alternative systems of working is something that all aspiring entrepreneurs should familiarize themselves with.

Quit Early and Quit Often | **Prof. Deepak Malhotra**
Unconventional career advice from a speech to grad-uating Harvard MBA students.

Shine Theory: Why Powerful Women Make the Greatest Friends | **Ann Friedman**
This powerful essay is something of a feminist ral-lying cry, and a reminder that (despite what society would have us think) other women are not your com-petition. Don't be duped – a rising tide lifts *all* boats.

The War of Art | **Steven Pressfield**
In a nutshell: how to push past creative block and get shit done.

WEBSITES TO BROWSE

Ask Polly | **nymag.com**
Heather Havrilesky's weekly agony aunt column for The Cut contains some of the most breathtakingly perceptive advice you'll ever read, for life inside and outside the office. Once you've worked your way through the online archives, check out her book *How to Be a Person in the World* for more.

Brain Pickings | **brainpickings.org**
An inventory of intellectual musings that draws inspiration from every corner of literature, this website is perfect for when you need new ways of looking at things.

The Dots | **the-dots.com**
A UK-based creative jobs board full of the kind of jobs you actually want! If you're on the hunt for a new job, don't sleep on this.

Fast Company | fastcompany.com
Stay up to date with the latest developments in business, creativity and tech – if startups are your thing, this is the place to be.

The Financial Diet | thefinancialdiet.com
A treasure trove of money advice that covers the personal finance side of things brilliantly. Warning: contains some serious real talk.

Harvard Business Review | hbr.org
Who says you need a fancy degree to start a business? Head to the HBR to pick up all the management, leadership, and, of course, business guidance you need, and get yourself an MBA on the cheap.

Women Who | womenwho.co
A platform for creative working women, consider this your go-to for career advice, fresh ideas and practical insights from cool, creative women who've 'been there'.

USEFUL TOOLS

Arena | Are.na
This beautifully designed website is great for collaborative projects where you're working in a team and want to share all of your references – be they images, files or links – in one place.

Evernote | evernote.com
This app allows you to collect and store all your ideas in one place, and sync them across your phone and computer. Less time getting organized = more time getting shit done.

Hunter | hunter.io
Need to get in touch with someone very busy and important but don't have their email address? Try this ingenious website for all your cold-emailing needs.

Moo | moo.com
Every mogul-in-the-making needs some professional-looking business cards. Get yours (and much more) at reasonable prices from this online stationery emporium.

Squarespace | squarespace.com
Probably the best website-building tool out there if you're in the market to launch a new business – not only does it look the part, it also makes setting up an online shop a breeze.

PLACES TO WORK: UK

Ace Hotel | London
The dedicated workspace in the London outpost's lobby is hugely popular with the freelance crowd, so get there early to bag yourself a seat at the communal long table – otherwise you'll have to settle for one of the (admittedly, very comfortable) sofas.

Barbican Centre | London
Dotted with comfy sofas, many of which are tucked away off the beaten track. Comes with free Wi-Fi and an in-house café serving drinks and snacks – what's not to love?

British Library Business and IP Centre National Network | UK-wide
Besides the ample study space available at its King's Cross location in London, the British Library also

operates centres in Leeds, Liverpool, Birmingham, Newcastle and Manchester, providing free resources and advice for budding entrepreneurs.

Central Library | Manchester
Whether you opt for the ground-floor seating area or settle down in the gorgeous domed Reading Room, you'll find peace and quiet aplenty in this recently refurbished Manchester icon. It also comes equipped with an on-site café for your caffeine needs.

National Art Library at the V&A | London
A public library open to all between Tuesdays and Saturdays, which (handily) is also a major reference library of fine and decorative arts dating back centuries.

Nordic Coffee Collective | Brighton
This gem lives up to its name by providing a) excellent coffee and b) stylish Scandi-chic decor. With fast, reliable Wi-Fi and an abundance of plug sockets, it's an excellent spot to set up camp for a few hours.

Timberyard | London
Good coffee, decent Wi-Fi and dedicated spaces to post up with your laptop. The Covent Garden

branch is a solid option for when you really need to focus.

TripKitchen | London
Part of the TripSpace group, this airy café is usually fairly quiet outside of lunchtimes. The events space next door also offers a daily roster of yoga classes, if you want to break up your day.

PLACES TO WORK: WORLDWIDE

Coffee Bar | San Francisco
This popular SoMa spot has ample table space and an industrious, buzzy vibe. Head upstairs for the best spots, far from the madding crowd.

New York Public Library | New York
If you enjoy working in beautiful surroundings (and who doesn't?), the NYPL's newly refurbished Rose Reading Room is the place for you – 'stunning' doesn't even come close.

The Springs | Los Angeles
This airy Downtown space is much more than just a place to work. With a roster of healthy food options,

an on-site yoga studio and a wellness centre, you'll probably end up doing much more than just working here.

Westberlin | Berlin
This self-proclaimed 'laptop-friendly' coffee shop follows through by providing separate working and reading areas for the Macbook brigade, as well as a huge selection of art and design magazines that are free to peruse.

PLACES TO INSPIRE: UK

Barbican Conservatory | London
A tropical oasis hidden away in the midst of a concrete jungle. Open most Sundays, but check in advance to be sure. Stop by the cinema afterwards and make a day of it.

Libreria | London
This cosy little bookshop organizes its books by theme, which often leads to the discovery of fairly unexpected connections. Expect a tightly curated selection – you'll find it impossible to leave without a book or two.

Modern Society | London
This beautiful boutique-cum-café on Redchurch Street feels like you're sitting in someone's sunlit garden. Come for the coffee, stay for the shopping.

Open Eye Gallery | Liverpool
An independent photography gallery located at the heart of the Liverpool Waterfront, round off your visit with a stroll past the city's most breathtaking architecture.

Tate Modern | London
Already a stalwart of London's cultural landscape, the Tate's newly built Switch House extension boasts more solo displays dedicated to female artists, as well as a viewing platform offering panoramic views of the city.

Turner Contemporary | Margate
Arguably the gem of Margate's cultural crown, this gallery is something of a mecca for art fans, and with good reason.

PLACES TO INSPIRE: WORLDWIDE

Droog | Amsterdam
This design-focused concept store is pretty hard to categorize, but well worth a visit. As well as the usual furniture pieces and home accessories one might expect, it also hosts exhibitions, occasional pop-ups and an outdoor 'Fairy Tale Garden'.

Goods For The Study | New York
Full of an artfully chosen selection of unique stationery, desk accessories and office furniture, head here to pimp out your workspace. An offshoot of the McNally Jackson bookstore a few blocks away (which is also worth a visit), this is stationery heaven.

Le Louxor | Paris
Located in an Art Deco building with a famously colourful history, this state-owned picture house steers away from commercial films in favour of world cinema, making it a great spot for film buffs.

NOTES

NOTES